We dedicate this book to Emma Labrado Colyer
and all the courageous Filipinas.

—Louis-Paul Heussaff

Published by
Louis-Paul Heussaff and
Supply Oilfield Services, Inc.
Pearlbank Center
146 Valero Street, Salcedo Village
Makati City
Philippines
www.sos.com.ph

Produced by
Editions Didier Millet
121 Telok Ayer Street #03-01
Singapore 068590
www.edmbooks.com

Philippines copyright © 2004 Supply Oilfield Services, Inc.

Printed in Singapore by Tien Wah Press

(FRONT AND BACK COVER) photographed by **Bobot Meru**
(PAGE 8) *Emma*
(PAGE 230) *Three Generations* by **Joanne Zapanta-Andrada**
(PAGE 236) *Flower* by **Louis-Paul Heussaff**

ISBN: 981-4155-12-8

Filipina

A Tribute to the Filipino Woman

Consultant photographer **George Tapan**
Designer **Vanessa Heussaff**
Project coordinator **Hélène Ratier**

Foreword by **Louis-Paul Heussaff**
Introduction by **F. Sionil Jose**

S.O.S., Inc.
L.-P. Heussaff

Contents

Foreword

Louis-Paul Heussaff
Chairman and CEO, Supply Oilfield Services, Inc.

Having made the Philippines my home for the last 25 years, I have grown accustomed to the Filipino way of life. I have learned that traffic jams are part of everyday routine, that Filipinos can spend hours at the mall just going around and buying nothing, that household helps are essential companions for the home, that Filipino time means always arriving behind schedule, that meal times are sacred hours for the family, and that Filipinos take breaks and snacks, every now and then. The list, as I am sure you know, could go on. But one more important thing I have observed is this: Filipinas are truly among the most beautiful women in the world.

My world revolves around Filipinas: my wife, my two daughters, my staff and my friends. Their personalities are as diverse as the 7,100 islands of the archipelago. Cynthia, my wife, was a talented dancer in her younger days. Now, she is a dedicated mother to our children and her love for them is unquestionable.

My eldest, Vanessa, is feisty, vocal and ambitious. If she wants to achieve something, she will pull out all the stops to realize her dream. There are times too when she can be very sweet.

Solenn, on the other hand, is her sister's opposite. She is easy-going, stylish and low-key. She finds simple pleasure in eating local staples like *tuyo* (dried fish) using her hands. Both my daughters are beautiful, intelligent and artistically inclined.

In my company, I am surrounded by Filipinas of all shapes and sizes (a.k.a. "My Little Army"). Some of them have been with me for more than a decade. They are faithful, hardworking and good-natured.

Such diversity is mirrored among the Filipinas today. They are a rich colorful tapestry of personalities and roles, of legacies and culture.

I couldn't let my 25 years in this country pass by without coming up with a second book, following the success of my first publishing venture *Philippines: Archipelago of Smiles.* In commemoration of Supply Oilfield Services, Inc.'s 25th anniversary, *Filipina: A Tribute to the Filipino Woman* is my gift to the women whose mere presence makes my life more interesting, colorful and bearable than usual.

This book is a bit atypical, for this was the result of the merging of talents of both professional and amateur photographers, the latter being participants of our nationwide photo contest which received 1,600 entries. We thank them for their invaluable contributions.

This selection of images pays homage to the *lolas, nanays, ates,* and *titas* of our everyday life, the businesswomen, artists, and leaders of our society.

Indeed the Filipina is a breathtaking image to behold. We hope that as you admire her in these pages, her true beauty will shine through: her elegance, her whimsical charm and her quiet strength. Without a doubt, the Filipina is the best asset of the Philippines.

Louis-Paul Heussaff

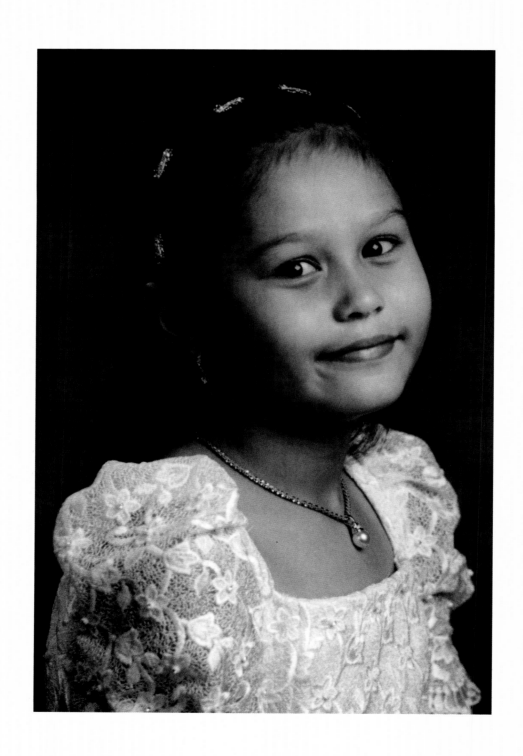

Introduction

F. Sionil Jose
Novelist, National Artist for Literature

How easy it is to exalt the Filipina, first as a man nurtured in my mother's womb and as a Filipino beholden to her grace. She comes to us as myth, a beauty that emerged from a length of bamboo that Bathala split open after he had created earth and high heaven. But soon enough, the myth became jewelled reality, the noble warrior in Princess Urdja, Gabriela Silang and Tandang Sora—women of stern courage who defended their birthright as all Filipinos should. She stands tall as beauty queen, as polished mannequin, and taller yet as concert diva, such as Jovita Fuentes who awed Europe in the '20s, and Lea Salonga as a Broadway star. But the inner shine and glory are in her professionalism as teacher, scientist, doctor and nurse—who was it who said that the American medical system would falter if all those Filipina nurses left?

Rizal creates an eternal heroine in Sisa, the long-suffering mother in the novel *Noli Me Tangere*. Sisa is now reality too in the thousands of Filipinas working abroad as domestics in the Middle East, Singapore and Hong Kong, and as entertainers in Japan. They are no less heroic than the warrior women who fought the Spaniards, Americans and Japanese. It is they who, with great sacrifice, keep the home fires burning. In the factories and on the farms, it is they who produce the goods that the capitalists sell, the food all of us eat and after doing these, they go home to mind the children and bind the family together.

Look closely at the faces of our women in these pages, young and old, peasant and aristocrat. In spite of the truculence of the times, the banality of our politics and the intransigence of our leaders, despair does not limn their eyes. Hope and joy reside in them, for these are Filipinas who will prevail, whose unhappy country will yet be redeemed by them.

F. Sionil Jose

In 1521, Magellan's chronicler Pigafetta extolled a queen in the Visayas as "young and beautiful; her mouth and nails were very red, while on her head she bore a large hat of palm leaves, like the tiara of the Pope." Indeed, the Filipina has since been recognized the world over for her sleek and regal image.

Elegance

Evidence is rife in our own art, on magazine covers, live on TV, from Amorsolo's portraits of country lasses bathing in streams to models conquering the international ramp, or beauty queens for whom grace has been the winning X-factor.

The soulfulness of the Filipina shines through, reflecting in her confidence the best of both worlds, East and West.

Her eloquence of spirit spells sheer elegance.

Alfred A. Yuson

Alfred A. Yuson

Marissa and the *sampaguita* (Philippine national flower) | **George Tapan**

Laeticia Ramos-Shahani, UNESCO Culture Committee Chairman |
Joanne Zapanta-Andrada

Vision from Davao | **George Tapan**

(PAGE 10)

A Mindanao State University student | **George Tapan**

Untitled | **Alberto D. Cruzada**

Colorful beauty | **Carlos I. Sampaga**

The smile | **Carlos I. Jose Jr.**

Model | George Tapan

In a beauty pageant | Joselito G. Arceta

Faces of fashion | courtesy of Jewelmer

Profile at sunset | George Tapan

Sonya in her garden | **George Tapan**

Solenn | **Louis-Paul Heussaff**

Lalaine Edson, model | **Wig Tysmans**

Vanessa | **Louis-Paul Heussaff**

(FOLLOWING PAGES)

Joey Mead, model and VJ | **Wig Tysmans**

Dalagete beauty, Cebu Island | **Wig Tysmans**

Cynthia Heussaff, Bayanihan group dancer | **Louis-Paul Heussaff**

Kuh Ledesma, singer | **George Tapan**

Magkaibigan (friends) | **Bien Bautista**

(PREVIOUS PAGES)

Harmony | **Bobot Meru**

Divas in New York City | **Andre Ner**

Gemma Cruz-Araneta, former
beauty queen and President of the
Heritage Conservation Society | **George Tapan**

Untitled | **Philippe 'Bo' Villanueva**

Kristin | Emil Davocol

Colonial | Franck M. Jimenez

Chaos | **Emil Davocol**

(PREVIOUS PAGES)

A quiet afternoon | **Emil Davocol**

Donita Rose, MTV VJ | **Raymund Isaac**

Graceful | **Leandro R. Valle**

Preparing for the moment | **Norman R. Gorecho**

Twins at Mount Santo Tomas | **RJ Fernandez**

Cruella de Pinta | **Andy Alvarez**

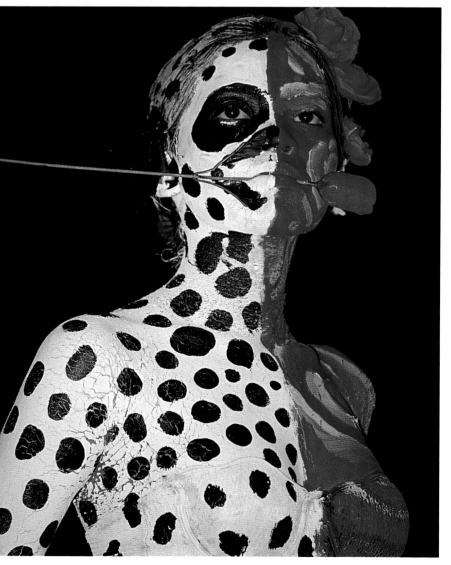

Lola (grandmother) Ebeng | **Bien Bautista**

Melanie Marquez, former Miss International | **Donald Tapan**

Portrait of a Visayan girl | **Eric Pasquier**

Candid | **George Tapan**

(PREVIOUS PAGES)

Amelia and Acel in El Nido | **George Tapan**

Jewelmer | **Philippe Venne**

Tradition and allure | **George Tapan**

Grace Nono, singer | **Manuel V. Fernandez**

Irma on Camiguin Island | **George Tapan**

The Ultimate Pearl | **Pierre-William Glenn**

(FOLLOWING PAGES)

Chin-Chin Gutierrez in Boracay | **George Tapan**

The most determined human beings I know are Filipinas: friends, ex-girlfriends, daughters. My sister. My mother. Let us add to that presidents, CEOs, film directors, musicians, traffic enforcers. There is something in the way the Filipina makes a meal, or makes a point, or makes love, the way she finally decides on matters of her home or her country, or her heart, and firmly goes the distance—with you or without you.

Determination

It is what makes you want to punch the wall with your fist, what makes you weep and makes you weak—her constant presence, her quiet strength, the soft, water-drop persistence of her enduring life and love.

Angelo R. Lacuesta

Veronica Pedrosa, CNN news anchor in Hong Kong | **Hoi-On Yeug**

(PAGE 60)

Muslim girl with pearl oyster | **Edwin Tuyay**

Loren Legarda, senator | **Edwin Tuyay**

Demonstrator on International Women's Day 2002 | **Victor D. Kintanar**

Fearless | Jacqueline M. Hernandez

Corazon Aquino, President of the Philippines (1986-1992) | **George Tapan**

Amelita Ramos, former Philippine First Lady | **George Tapan**

At the service of the Filipino people | **Bobot Meru**

Jocelyn A. Patrimonio, Philippine Air Force pilot | **Victor D. Kintanar**

Lieutenant Virginia P. Nepomuceno, pride of the
Philippine Air Force | **George Tapan**

Lieutenant-Colonel Ramona Palabrica-Go, first woman battalion
commander of the Philippine Air Force | **George Tapan**

(PREVIOUS PAGES)

Gemith Gemparo, fashion model and pilot | **Joanne Zapanta-Andrada**

On the field | **George Tapan**

Women of Supply Oilfield Services, Inc. | **George Tapan**

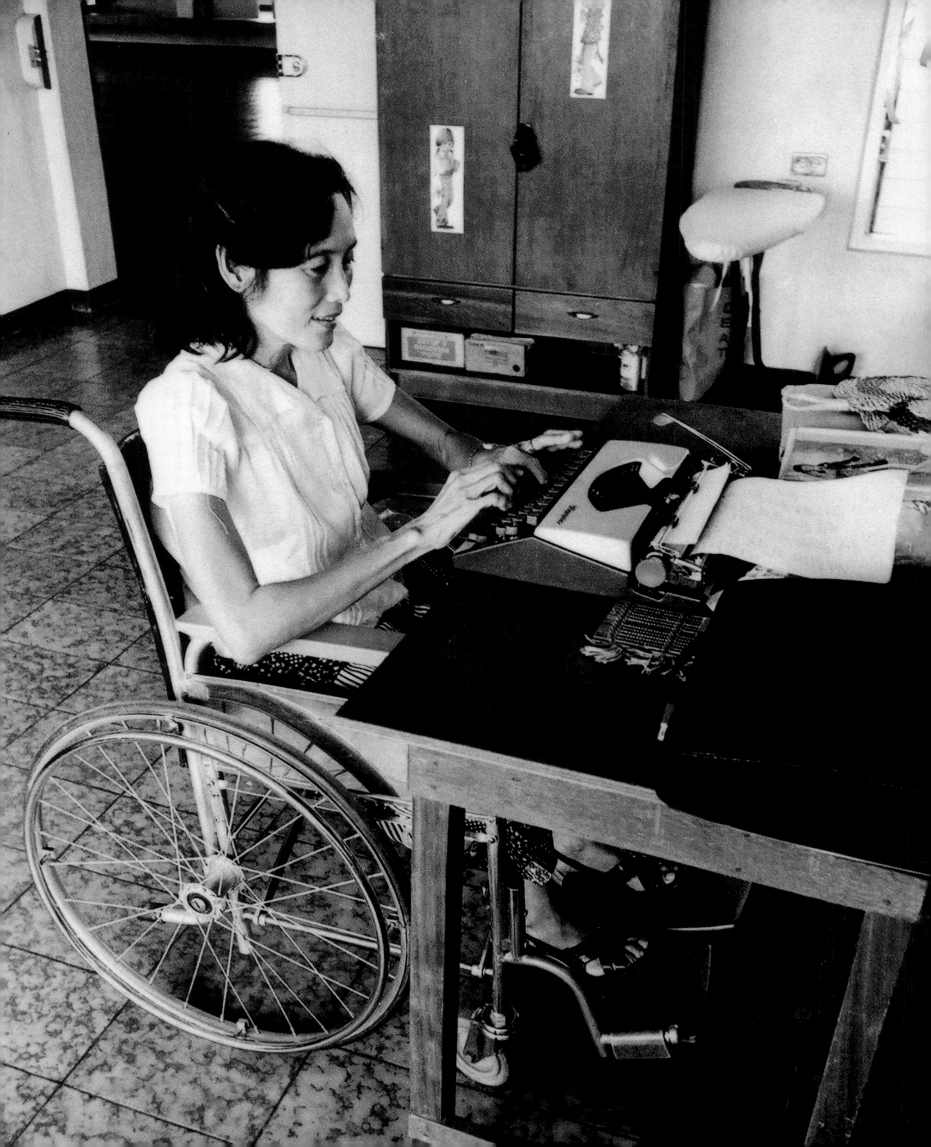

Untitled | **Donald Tapan**

(PREVIOUS PAGES)

Rachel Abilla, firefighter | **George Tapan**

Joanne Rae-Ramirez, newspaper editor | **Joanne Zapanta-Andrada**

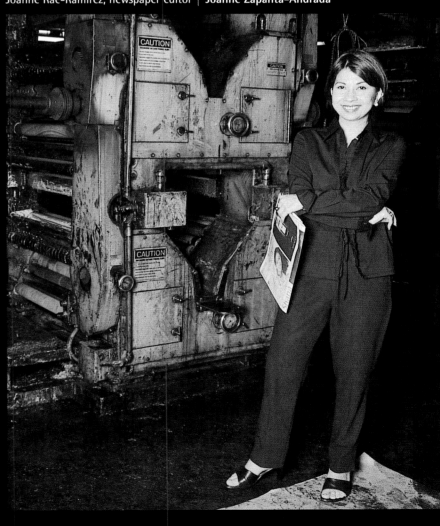

Lulu Tan Gan, fashion designer | **George Tapan**

Myrza Sison, editor-in-chief of *Cosmopolitan* (Philippines) | **Paolo Pineda**

Barkada (buddies) I │ **Bobot Meru**

Barkada (buddies) II │ **Bobot Meru**

Game cock breeder | **Jun Barrameda**

Motorcyclist | **Bobot Meru**

Rhythmic gymnast | **Edwin Bellosillo**

Contortionist | **Joe Galvez**

Joy Zapanta, street-fighting aficionado | **Joanne Zapanta-Andrada**

Josephine So, Miss Great Body 2002–2003 | **Louis-Paul Heussaff**

Elma Muros, the winner | **Revoli S. Cortez**

Passion and agony | **Edwin Bellosillo**

Christine Jacob, South East Asian Games and
Olympic swimmer | **George Tapan**

Mikee Cojuangco, equestrian champion | **Ramon Vecina**

Jayvie Agojo, junior golf champion | **Joey Mendoza**

Goalie | Jörg Schifferer

Dragon boat crew | Levi Nayahangan

Working underwater | **Gutsy Tuason**

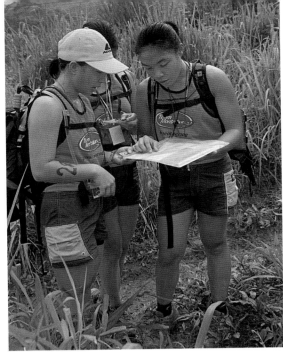

Adventure racers | **Levi Nayahangan**

Kathy Leen C. Perez, *arnis* and taekwondo instructor | **George Tapan**

Elma Muros, 35 gold medals in 21 years of athletic competition | **Edwin Tuyay**

Mae Young, Ultimate Frisbee player | **George Tapan**

(PREVIOUS PAGES)

Pushing the limits | **Antonio 'Myk' Miguel Jr.**

Cave explorer | **Levi Nayahangan**

(FOLLOWING PAGES)

Mountaineer | **George Tapan**

In a country where natural disasters such as typhoons, earthquakes and volcano eruptions are common occurrences, and which has experienced the vagaries of colonialism three times in its short history, the figure of the loving and devoted Filipina is akin to a ray of sunshine, the *amihan* (wind from the east) or the land itself. An inherent part of her character that cannot be overlooked is her exceptional capacity for love and devotion.

Devotion

The images of popular culture dictate that the former quality is magnified and the latter given scant, if any, notice. Yet the heart of Maria Clara beats not only with love for Crisostomo, but also with devotion to her duty. Without the latter, she would not be a true Filipina, and she would not be Maria Clara.

César Ruiz Aquino

A moment of tenderness on a boat trip | **Gil Nartea**

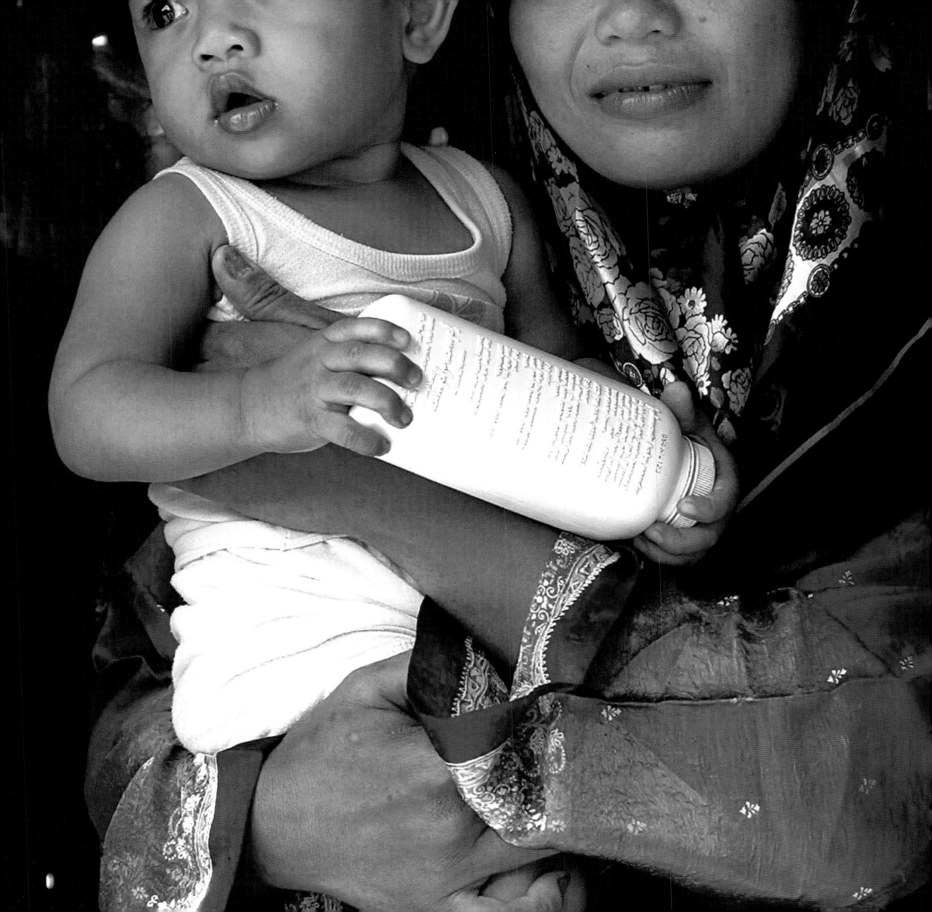

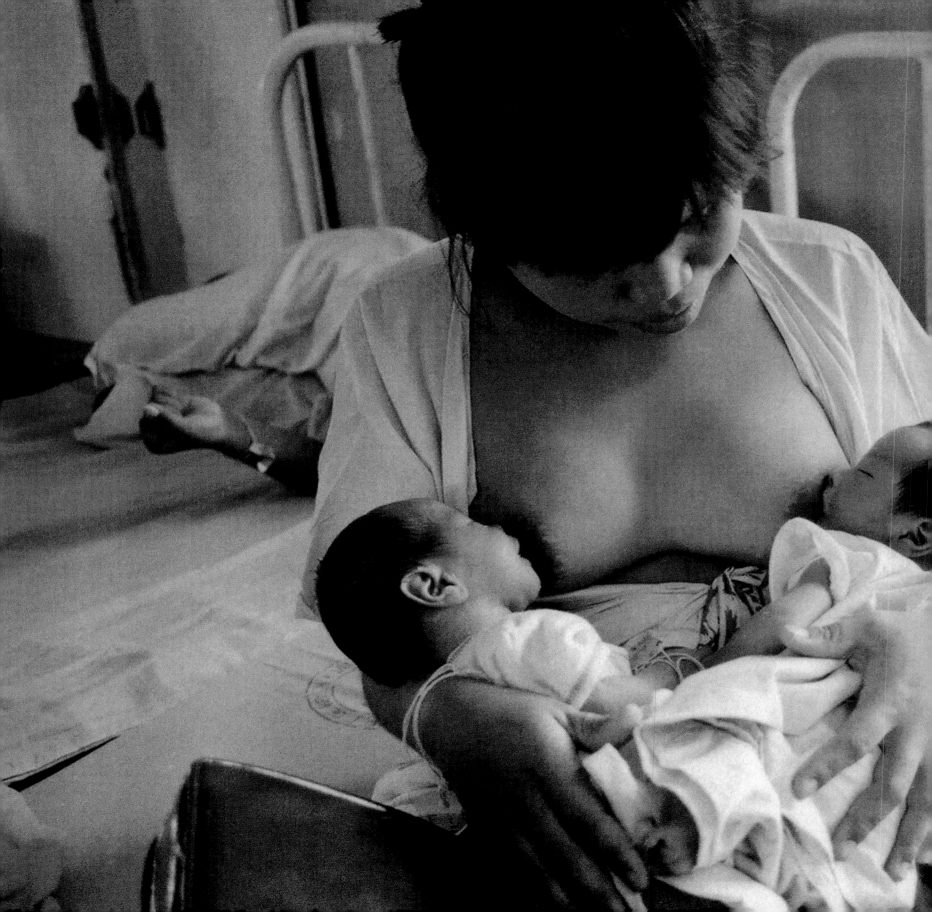

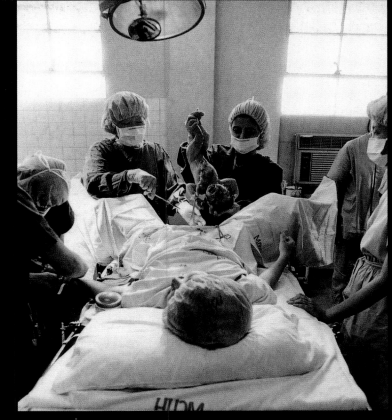

Child-birth | **Donald Tapan**

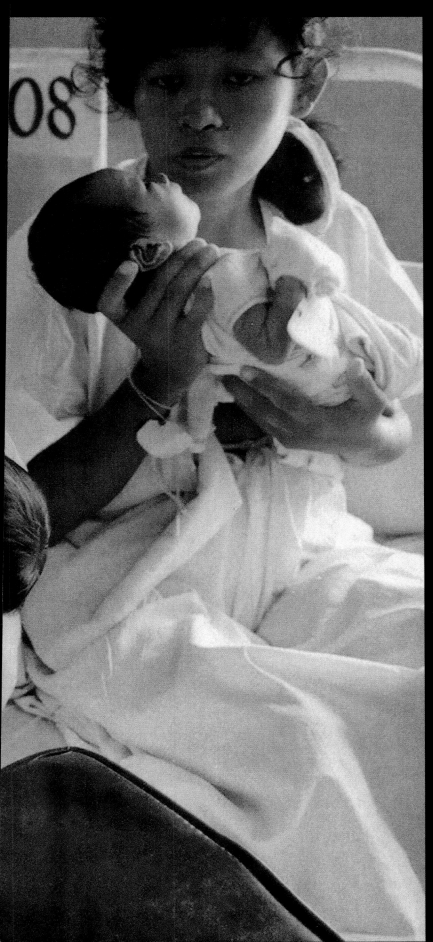

Room for two | **Sonny Yabao**

Devotion

Gloria Diaz, mother and Miss Universe 1969 | George Tapan

Nina Yap, pre-school teacher | Joanne Zapanta-Andrada

Happy family in Zambales | **Revoli S. Cortez**

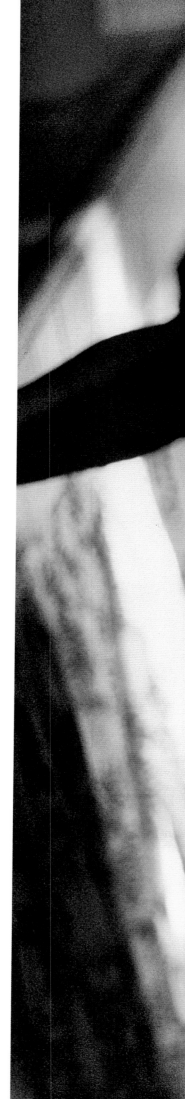

The embrace | **Henri E. Nanini**

(FOLLOWING PAGES)

Badjaos (sea gypsies) fetching water | **Gil Nartea**

Hardship | **Patricio Roel A. Pira**

Toiling at a tobacco farm | **George Tapan**

Beach vendor | **George Tapan**

Weaver | **Roberto S. Mendoza**

Untitled | **Ruben Abaya Pagaduan**

Story time | Ernesto J. Villanueva Jr.

Holding tight | Ronnie Poblacion

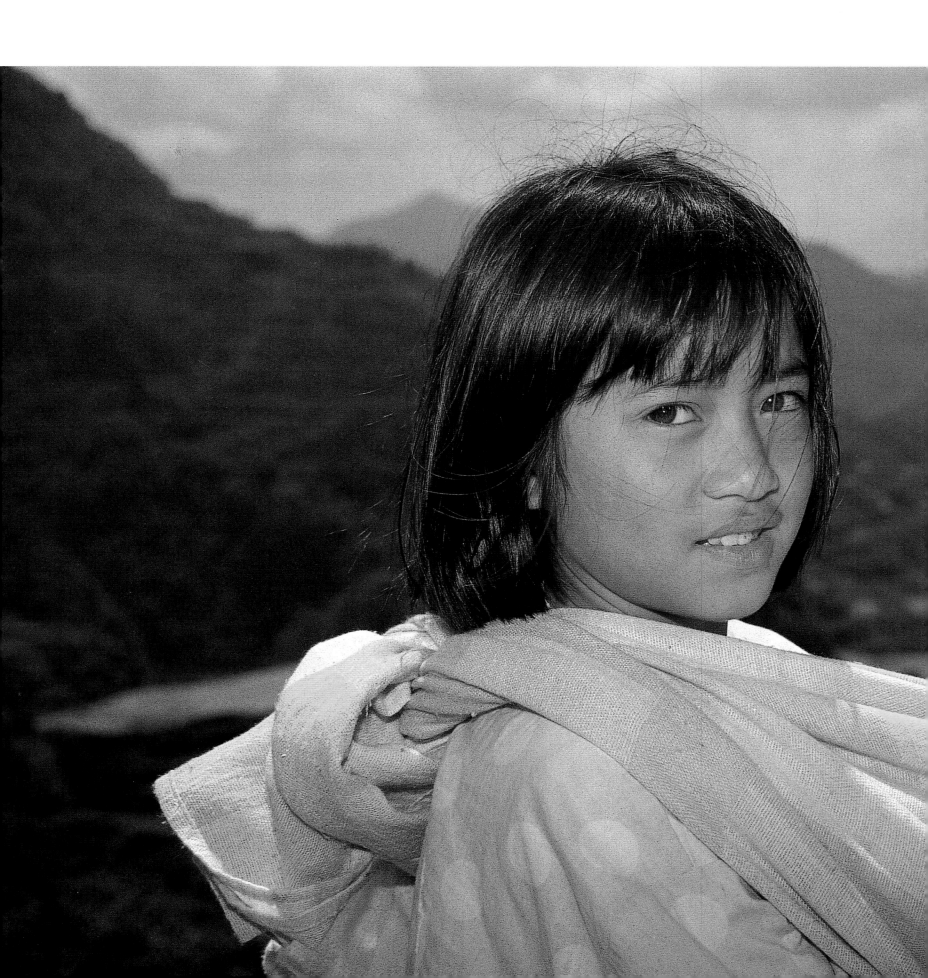

Helping *lola* (grandmother) | Leah M. Castillo

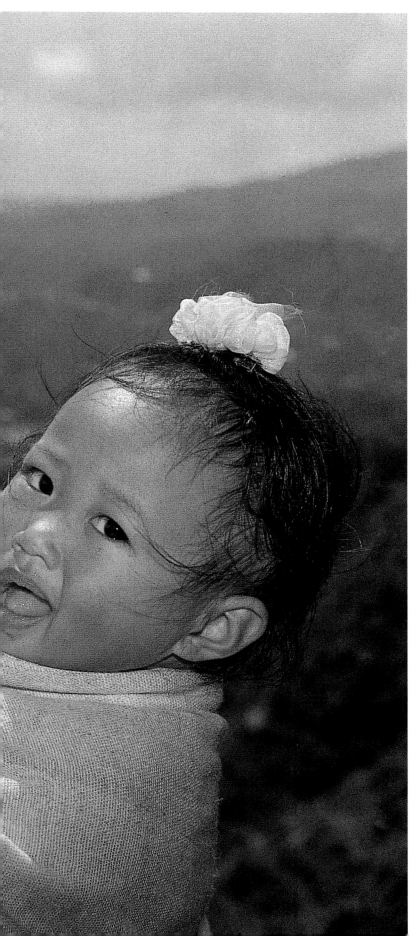

Siblings in the Mountain Province | Espiridion M. Enriquez

Day by day | **Maria Luisa Roldan**

Untitled | **Ignacio P. San Gabriel Jr.**

A lifetime on Batanes Island | **Maria Luisa Roldan**

Home | **Joey de Castro**

(FOLLOWING PAGES)

Untitled | **Ramon I. Castillo**

Sisters in Sabtang, Batanes Island | **Bien Bautista**

Sisterhood | **Louis-Paul Heussaff**

(PREVIOUS PAGES)

For a brighter future | **Rhoda R. Orbeta**

At a prayer rally in Luneta Park | Revoli S. Cortez

Piety | Ignacio P. San Gabriel Jr.

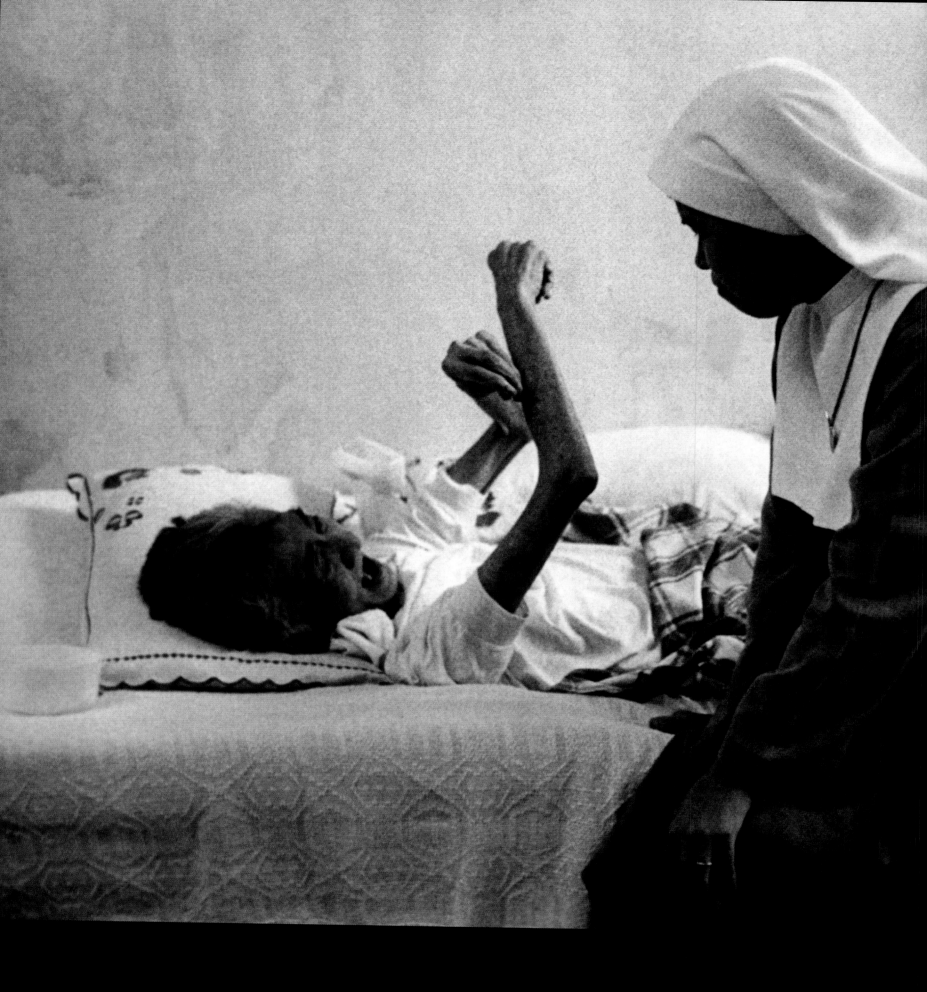

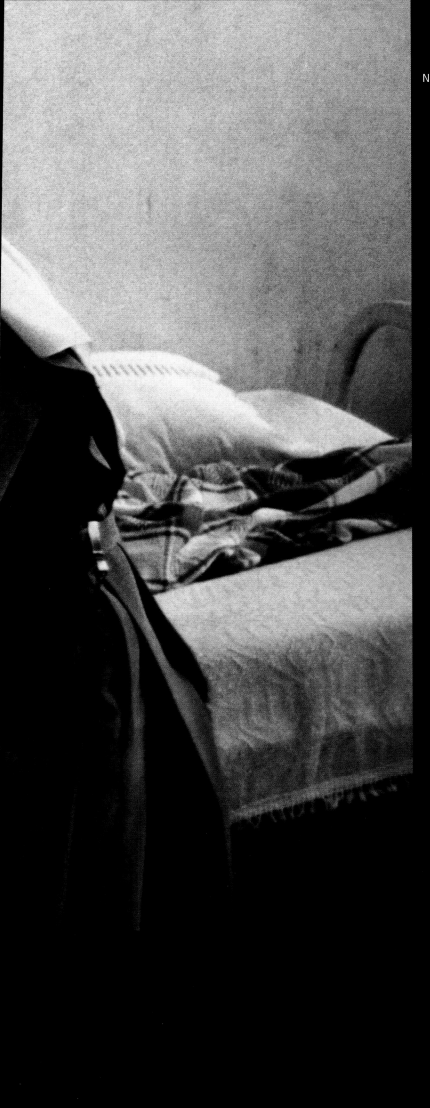

Nun tending to a patient | **Sonny Yabao**

Lifesaver | **Jay Gicaro Estoya**

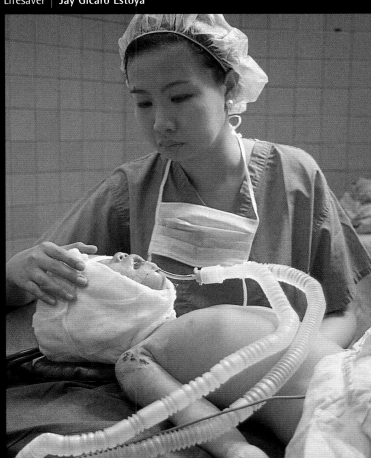

World War II veterans' wives in Bataan | **George Tapan**

The vocation | Leonardo F. de Andres

Call for peace | Joseph Agcaoili

Together in Smokey Moutain | **Pierre-Henri Lefebvre**

(PREVIOUS PAGES)

Angels | **Sonny Yabao**

Justice Josefina Guevara-Salonga | **Joanne Zapanta-Andrada**

Patience | **Sonny Yabao**

Manabo tribeswoman | **Edwin Tuyay**

Descendants of Maranaw royalty | **George Tapan**

(FOLLOWING PAGES)

From one generation to another of T'Bolis women | **George Tapan**

The Filipina cares deeply for and will protect those whom she loves at any cost. She listens keenly to her intuition, able to distinguish friend from foe and opportunity from disaster. She will listen but heed only those words which she deems wise or meaningful.

Sensibility

She is always searching for happiness and may find that she has to pay dearly for her desire, but her soul is as hardy as it is ambitious, and she will prevail, restored and reaffirmed, filled with hope and eager to seek fulfillment anew. She is a proud creature and will not be defeated, except by God and fate. She is devout and will kiss the divine hand which guides her life, but in her earthly existence, it is her hand that guides her family and nation.

Jose Dalisay

Lea Salonga | **George Tapan**

(PAGE 156)

Joanne Zapanta-Andrada, model and photographer | **George Tapan**

Lucita Soriano, actress | **Rosemarie B. Razon**

Ednah Ledesma, Philippine dance champion |
George Tapan

Saxophonist | **Andy Maluche**

Lisa Macuja, ballerina | **George Tapan**

Choir | **Antonio Z. Rojas Jr.**

Jaya, singer | **Raymund Issac**

Sovietskaya Bacud, model | **Louis-Paul Heussaff**

Pops Fernandez, singer | **Raymund Isaac**

The contestant | **Antonio Z. Rojas Jr.**

Dancers in a jeepney | **Ignacio P. San Gabriel Jr.**

Ai Ai de las Alas, comedienne | **Raymund Issac**

Mia Urquico, fashion designer | **Joanne Zapanta-Andrada**

(PREVIOUS PAGES)

The festival spirit | **Alan Borras**

Burdadera (embroiderer) | **Donald Tapan**

Elena | **Bien Bautista**

Anita Magsaysay-Ho, painter with daughter Doris,
business executive and columnist | **George Tapan**

Jessie C. Sincioco, chef | **George Tapan**

Anna Sy, architect and interior designer | **George Tapan**

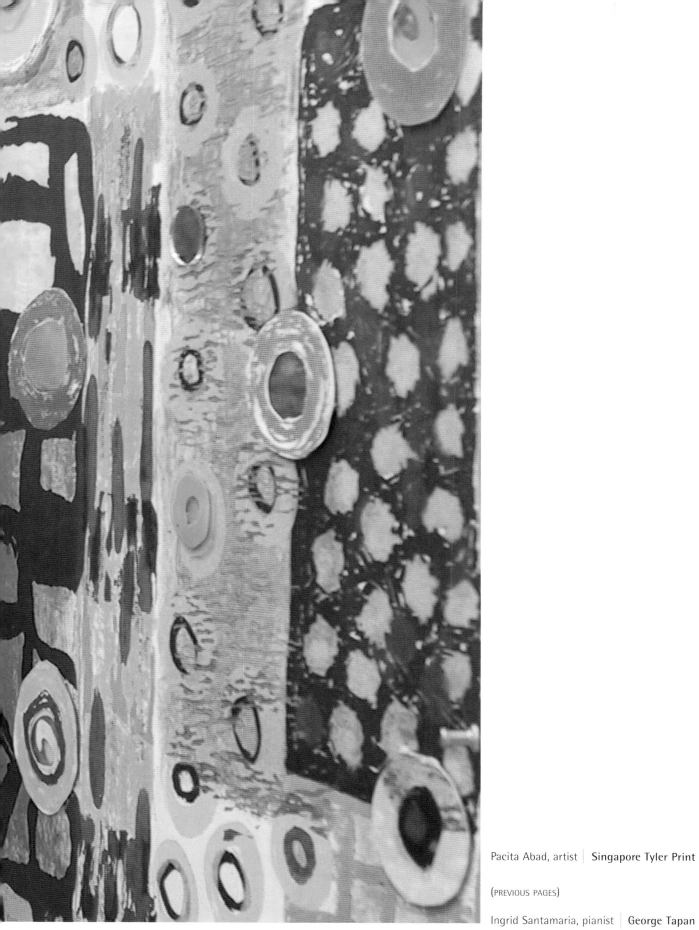

Pacita Abad, artist | Singapore Tyler Print Institute

(PREVIOUS PAGES)

Ingrid Santamaria, pianist | George Tapan

Solenn and a tarsier in Bohol | **Derek Ramsey**

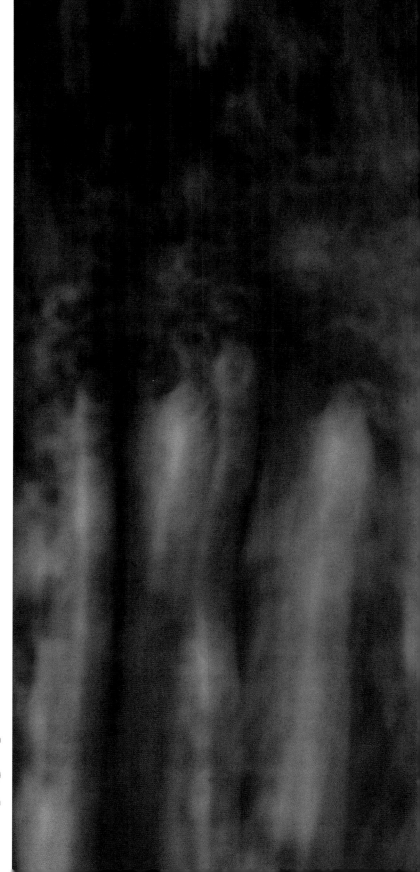

Hannah with *lanzones* (local fruit) | **George Tapan**

(FOLLOWING PAGES)

The ecstatic Filipina in Paris | **George Tapan**

Whenever you look into the eyes of a Filipina, you will instantly feel the tropical warmth of friendship.

Whenever you look into her eyes, you will see the glint of compassion and humor singing morning songs,

Individuality

When you look into her eyes, you will feel the sensual radiance of one humbled before an august presence,

When you look into her eyes, you will see the star still shining that once led the ancient Magi long ago to the humble stables,

Look into her eyes, you will feel her submission to your whim and desire,

Look into her eyes, you will discern the deep color of loyalty,

Look into her eyes, she will feed you as wife and mother, bear you children, and care for you whenever illness visits; she will organize your wardrobe, room, and home,

And after she has done everything to comfort and keep you warm,

Look into her eyes. You will then most quietly know that she is the boss.

Nonon Padilla

Flower farmer in Benguet | **Sonny Yabao**

Sampaguita (Philippine national flower) vendor | **Jun Barrameda**

(PAGE 192)

Bea Serrano, primary school student | **Joanne Zapanta-Andrada**

Tausug woman, Tawi-Tawi | **Gil Nartea**

Selling rice cakes in Cebu | **George Tapan**

Handicraft makers from the Visayas Islands | **Gil Nartea**

A jubilant Metro-Aide | Reynaldo Mondez

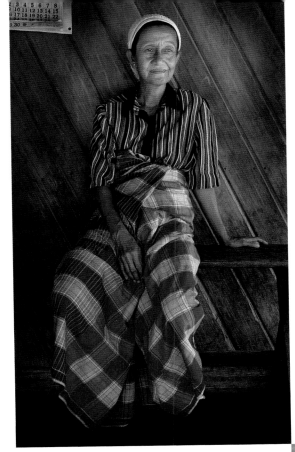

An elderly Muslim woman | **Gil Nartea**

Patriot | **Reynaldo R. Dalmacio**

Ifugao woman, north Luzon | **Raniel Jose M. Castaneda**

Badjao (sea gypsy) women of Tawi-Tawi | **Gil Nartea**

Diving for a living | Joaquin B. Ruste

(PREVIOUS PAGES)

Ageless | Joselito G. Arceta

Nature lover | George Tapan

Keeper of the Bukidnon tribe's traditions | **Eric Pasquier**

An Ivatan tribeswoman, Batanes Island | **Jun Barrameda**

Full of life | **Alberto D. Cruzada**

(PREVIOUS PAGES)

T'Bolis women at Lake Sebu, Cotabato | **Eric Pasquier**

Celebrating Mardi Gras in Greenbelt, Makati | **Andy Maluche**

Melanie Marquez, model and actress | **Donald Tapan**

(PREVIOUS PAGES)

Youthful laughter | **Joanne Zapanta-Andrada**

Tessa Prieto-Valdez, columnist and fashion chameleon |
Joanne Zapanta-Andrada

Shoe-maker | **Jun Barrameda**

Potter | **Bobot Meru**

Mechanic | **Joanne Zapanta-Andrada**

Amongst the reels | **Bobot Meru**

Policewoman in Cebu | **George Tapan**

Traffic enforcer | **Reynaldo Mondez**

Rebel | **Louis-Paul Heussaff**

Nica, political science graduate | **Jerome M. Palma**

(FOLLOWING PAGES)

Mestizas in Forbes Park | **Bobot Meru**

Afterword

Carmen N. Pedrosa
Columnist for the *Philippine Star*

A Different Book on the Filipino Woman

When Louis-Paul Heussaff asked me to write the summary for his book *Filipina: A Tribute to the Filipino Woman,* I thought, "Oh no, not another book on the same theme again." I asked to see the pictures and text and was pleasantly surprised. It was not the run-of-the-mill book on Filipino women, which usually ends up with pictures of Filipino women who were either beautiful or prominent with tiresome text. The book uses both known and unknown women, but always beautifully photographed, to symbolize a woman's virtues. For example, there's a photograph showing only a model's neck and a string of pearls in the Elegance chapter. The book focuses our attention on the virtues admittedly sometimes disproportionately possessed by Filipino women. But rather than focus on the women themselves the book, using photographic excellence, is about elegance, determination, devotion, sensibility and individuality. The result was a beautiful book of photographs and unobtrusive text. The title *Filipina: A Tribute to the Filipino Woman* is delightfully incidental.

I should perhaps end this conclusion with what to me is worth noting, that it was a project conceived by a man. But to paraphrase a sage, "A woman is too wise to crow that she has won the battle of the sexes."

Carmen N. Pedrosa

Acknowledgements

For their precious assistance and support throughout the *Filipina* project, many thanks to:

Brian Lim book design and technical consultant
Rose Policarpio, Christie Rose Ang, Senen Lazaro, Nilda and Dennis Leyva
Daniel Carpentier, Louis Vergeon
M. Ramon A. Recto President, Supply Oilfield Services, Inc.
Managers and staff of Supply Oilfield Services, Inc.
The Heussaff family (Mdm. Cynthia, Vanessa, Solenn and Erwan)
Agerico T. Paras and **Siddhartha JP III S. Penaredondo** attorneys

For supporting the *Filipina* photo contest, warmest thanks to:

Embassy of France
Renée Veyret, Ambassador
Franck Hébert, Counsellor for Cooperation and Cultural Affairs

Air France
Louis Vergeon, General Manager

Department of Tourism
Dick Gordon, Secretary
Jazmin C. Esguerra, Officer-in-Charge (Bureau of International Tourism Promotion)

Globe Telecom
Gerard Ablaza, President

Konica Film
Benito Tan, President
Cecile Agustin, Marketing Manager

Judges of the *Filipina* photo contest:

Renée Veyret Ambassador, Embassy of France
Franck Hébert Counsellor for Cooperation and Cultural Affairs, Embassy of France
Jazmin C. Esguerra Officer-in-Charge, Bureau of International Tourism Promotion
Gemma Cruz-Araneta President, Heritage Conservation Society
Cynthia Heussaff Supply Oilfield Services, Inc.
Caroline Cliff British Women's Association
Jeremy Cliff Managing Director, Shell Philippines Exploration B.V.
Louis Vergeon General Manager, Air France
Mayenne Carmona columnist, *Philippine Star*
Cecile Agustin Marketing Manager, Konica Film
Daniel Carpentier PDP Digital Inc.
Fred Baldemor sculptor

Photographers

For making this book possible and for their beautiful work, special thanks to:

Our *Filipina* team of professional photographers who collaborated on this project with much enthusiasm and dedication:

George Tapan, Joanne Zapanta-Andrada, Raymund Isaac, Wig Tysmans, Bien Bautista, Gil Nartea, Jun Barrameda, Edwin Tuyay, Donald Tapan, Emil Davocol, Bobot Meru, Sonny Yabao

The various photographers who generously contributed to this book:

Louis-Paul Heussaff, Eric Pasquier, Pierre-William Glenn, Gutsy Tuason, Andy Maluche, Jörg Schifferer, Joseph Agcaoili, Edwin Bellosillo, Levi Nayahangan, Philippe Venne, Eddy Boy Escudero, Joey Mendoza, Paolo Pineda, Hoi-On Yeug, Derek Ramsey

The photographers who joined the *Filipina* photo contest:

Alberto D. Cruzada, Carlos I. Jose Jr., Carlos I. Sampaga, RJ Fernandez, Joselito G. Arceta, Leandro R. Valle, Norman R. Gorecho, Carlos B. Carlo, Manuel V. Fernandez, Franck M. Jimenez, Andre Ner, Philippe 'Bo' Villanueva, Andy Alvarez, Victor D. Kintanar, Joe Galvez, Antonio 'Myk' Miguel Jr., Jacqueline M. Hernandez, Ramon Vecina, Revoli S. Cortez, Henri E. Nanini, Leah M. Castillo, Ernesto J. Villanueva Jr., Rhoda R. Orbeta, Espiridion M. Enriquez, Jay Gicaro Estoya, Pierre-Henri Lefebvre, Roberto S. Mendoza, Ronnie Poblacion, Ramon I. Castillo, Maria Luisa Roldan, Patricio Roel A. Pira, Ignacio P. San Gabriel Jr., Leonardo F. de Andres, Joey de Castro, Ruben Abaya Pagaduan, Reynaldo Mondez, Raniel Jose M. Castaneda, Reynaldo R. Dalmacio, Jerome M. Palma, Pacita Tiong, Joaquin B. Ruste, Antonio Z. Rojas Jr., Josefino P. Marcelino, Rosemarie B. Razon, Alan Borras

Writers

For bringing their insights on capturing the essence of the Filipina:

F. Sionil Jose, Carmen N. Pedrosa, Johanna Francisco, Alfred A. Yuson, Jose Dalisay, Angelo Lacuesta, César Ruiz Aquino, Nonon Padilla

Special thanks

Our deepest appreciation also goes to:

Jewelmer International Corporation, M. Branellec and M. Cojuangco
Cosmopolitan (Philippines)
Studio 58
Viva Records
Genesis Talent Agency
CNN Hong Kong
Backroom, M. Boy Abunda
Singapore Tyler Print Institute
Restaurant Le Soufflé, Ortigas
Restaurant Sonya's Garden, Tagaytay
Ms Chin-Chin Gutierrez
The Tapan family (George, Maria Luisa, Hannah, Harold and Harvey)
Makati Central Fire Station
The Philippine Air Force
GJS: thanks for the inspiration

Index of photographers

Numbers indicate pages where pictures appear